IMAGES
of America

TORRANCE
POLICE DEPARTMENT

The Torrance Police Department has used four primary shoulder emblems in its history.

ON THE COVER: Seen in this 1952 image is the traffic division with, from left to right, Patrolman Dave Cook, Patrolman Hughy "Buck" Ingram, Sgt. G. S. "Bill" Evans, Assistant Chief Willard "Pop" Haslam, Patrolman Harold "Zeke" Trezise, Patrolman Don Nash, Patrolman Jim Thompson, and Patrolman William "Bob" Lewis. Lewis and Cook are on their private motorcycles and are wearing the old-style tan motorcycle uniforms and soft caps used for funeral escorts. The three-wheeled motorcycle in the center was used for parking enforcement. (Courtesy Torrance Police Department Library.)

IMAGES
of America

TORRANCE
POLICE DEPARTMENT

John Prins

ARCADIA
PUBLISHING

Published by Arcadia Publishing
Charleston SC, Chicago IL, Portsmouth NH, San Francisco CA

Printed in the United States of America

Library of Congress Catalog Card Number: 2007925814

For all general information contact Arcadia Publishing at:
Telephone 843-853-2070
Fax 843-853-0044
E-mail sales@arcadiapublishing.com
For customer service and orders:
Toll-Free 1-888-313-2665

Visit us on the Internet at www.arcadiapublishing.com

This book is dedicated to the men and women who have worn or are
still wearing the uniform of the Torrance Police Department as well as to
TPD's dedicated civilian personnel, without whom we could not do our
job. In particular, I would like to dedicate this book to:

Sgt. William Robert Lewis, end of watch August 23, 1959
Officer David Noel Seibert, end of watch August 10, 1967
Officer Gary Elton Rippstein, end of watch December 22, 1968
Officer Thomas Joseph Keller, end of watch April 17, 1986
Crossing Guard Hazel Kenney, end of watch December 17, 1986
May there never be others!

Last but not least, this book is dedicated to the citizens of Torrance. It
is largely as a result of their constant support throughout the years that
the Torrance Police Department has been able to provide quality police
service to the community.

CONTENTS

Foreword   6

Acknowledgments   8

Introduction   9

1.   The Early Years: 1921–1930   11

2.   The Great Depression Years: 1930–1940   15

3.   World War II and the Postwar Years: 1940–1950   23

4.   Law Enforcement in the "All-America City:" 1950–1960   37

5.   Reorganization: 1960–1970   59

6.   Stability and Growth: 1970–1980   85

7.   A New Facility: 1980–1990   93

8.   Excellence through Teamwork: 1990–2006   115

FOREWORD

Throughout several decades of dedicated public service, many fine men and women have contributed great insight and guidance into shaping the Torrance Police Department. The success of our organization can only be attributed to the outstanding quality and dedication of each and every person who has served as a member of the Torrance Police Department. For over 86 years, this department has been committed to keeping our city safe by taking a proactive approach to policing while at the same time exemplifying excellence through teamwork.

Within these pages are the names and photographs of many of the heroes and heroines who have worked tirelessly to make our department what it is today. They were ordinary men and women—fathers and mothers, husbands and wives, sons and daughters, brothers and sisters, friends and colleagues. It is with great pride that I can say because of their efforts throughout the years, we continue to be recognized as one of the preeminent law enforcement agencies in California and beyond.

The history of policing in Torrance evolved through the years to keep pace with the growth of our community. We continue to adapt and evolve to meet the unique challenges we face today and into the future. Today the Torrance Police Department provides law enforcement to 142,621 Torrance residents encompassing an area of 21 square miles. To accomplish this, the department employs approximately 242 police officers and detectives and more than 100 civilian support-staff personnel. Their commitment to public safety and the community we serve is second to none.

Torrance officers, both retired and active, firmly believe they are members of the finest police department in the nation. There are none better or more dedicated to their profession than the members of this agency. It is truly my honor to dedicate this book to all members, past and present, of the Torrance Police Department.

—Chief of Police John J. Neu
Torrance, California, 2007

John J. Neu was appointed chief of police on October 10, 2006. Chief Neu began his career in law enforcement with the Pasadena Police Department and transferred to the Torrance Police Department on August 29, 1985, rising to the rank of captain by July 2002. Chief Neu was born in Redondo Beach and was raised in Torrance, where he attended West Torrance High School. Chief Neu has established Focus Based Policing as well as the supervisory development course currently in use for training new supervisors. Chief Neu also implemented the department's latest recruitment program, which incorporates a multimedia approach using current technologies.

ACKNOWLEDGMENTS

I set out with this book to illustrate 86 years of history of one of the finest law enforcement agencies around. My goal was to depict the diversity, professionalism, and teamwork for which the Torrance Police Department (TPD) is known. The information in this book has come from several sources: logbooks, newspaper articles, scrapbook clippings, and personal accounts. I owe a great debt of gratitude to the following people. Without their assistance, this book would not have been possible.

I would like to thank, first and foremost, retired TPD lieutenant Dave Cook for his tireless assistance in filling in the gaps and identifying faces in photographs. Dave unfortunately passed away on July 30, 2007, before this book was published. Rest in peace, sir! Retired captain Jim Weyant, the unofficial historian of the department, provided invaluable past research into TPD's history. Former TPD patrolman Jay Stroh, a true gentleman, supplied priceless photographs of and information on his father, Chief John Stroh. Retired lieutenants Wally Murker, Paul Nowatka, and Charlie Oates and retired sergeants Mel Bennett and Ray Ouellette provided cooperation and assistance. A special thanks goes to Aggie Barnett, wife of former TPD patrolman Willard "Barney" Barnett, and to Jack Johnson, son of former TPD lieutenant Swayne Johnson, for the historical photographs. Sam Gnerre, chief librarian of the *Daily Breeze*, and the management of the newspaper allowed me to use certain historical photographs.

The following current and retired Torrance Police Department personnel donated numerous images, not all of which could be included because of space constraints: Marsha Barnet, Leonard Beal, Bob Bowman, Kathy Diaz, Myriam Dowdy, Craig Durling, Jack and Maxine Hahn, Dave Hancock, Bob Kammerer, Penny Koenig, Kevin Kreager, Gary Lacroix, Dave Marsden, Jason McDonald, Dan Murray, Dexter Nelms, Jim Randall, Larry Robinson, Greg Satterfield, Charlene Spradlin (wife of "Sprad"), Bob Such, Mary Temple, and Carol Wright.

Chief Jim Herren and Chief John Neu and their command staffs gave me the go-ahead and allowed me to work on this project.

Thanks to Jerry Roberts, my editor from Arcadia Publishing, for his professional assistance.

Finally, my wife, Maria, allowed me to sacrifice many hours in order to complete this book.

INTRODUCTION

The city of Torrance is located approximately 17 miles southwest of downtown Los Angeles in a region known as the South Bay section of Los Angeles County. Torrance encompasses an area of approximately 21 square miles and has a population of 142,621 inhabitants, making it the 6th largest municipality in Los Angeles County and the 34th largest in the state of California. The city is bordered on the southwest by approximately one mile of Pacific Ocean beachfront, on the west by the city of Redondo Beach, on the north by the city of Lawndale, on the east by the cities of Gardena and Los Angeles (Harbor Gateway), on the southeast by the city of Lomita, and on the south by the cities of Rolling Hills Estates and Palos Verdes Estates.

Torrance developed in the early 1900s as a planned garden-industrial community. The plan provided a balance between industrial, commercial, and residential uses. The city incorporated on May 12, 1921, one year after the death of its founder and namesake, Jared Sydney Torrance, with a land area of 3.8 square miles and a population of 1,800. Rapid growth occurred during the 1950s and 1960s, and the majority of the housing stock was built during those two decades. The city is now largely built out and has had a relatively stable population for the last two decades.

The maintenance of law and order in the community prior to incorporation was the responsibility of the County of Los Angeles. During these early years, a constable from Lomita by the name of Ed Voris served in the capacity of night watchman for the Torrance community.

The Torrance Police Department dates to May 23, 1921, when city trustees appointed Ben Olsen as the first city marshal and shortly thereafter hired Byron Anderson as night watchman. Their efforts were devoted to dealing with thieves, keeping the peace, and catching speeding motorists. For unknown reasons, Ben Olsen submitted his resignation as city marshal on December 13, 1921, yet chose to stay on as a member of the department. He was succeeded by night watchman Byron Anderson, who became city marshal/chief of police and served in that capacity until November 24, 1924.

Lester Stanley was appointed motorcycle officer on January 16, 1923, followed by a second motorcycle officer, Stanley Abbott, later that same year. Chief Anderson was using his personal car to transport prisoners and complained about this to the city's board of trustees, but it wasn't until the middle of 1923 that an Essex car was purchased. William Phillips was appointed night watchman on May 14, 1923, and another night watchman by the name of I. Z. Thorpe was hired on June 2, 1924. Also in 1924, the first policeman's ball was held in the Legion Hall.

On November 10, 1924, Loren F. Patterson, an investigator with the Los Angeles County District Attorney's Office, was appointed city marshal/chief of the department, staying on until May 5, 1926. Among other things, Chief Patterson and his police force rigidly enforced federal Prohibition laws.

Chief Gerald M. Calder followed Patterson as chief of police and served the city in that capacity for over 12 years, until July 1, 1938. He would stay on as captain until April 1947.

From these humble beginnings, the Torrance Police Department has grown into the fourth largest municipal law enforcement agency in Los Angeles County. Its position as the anchoring police force of the South Bay section of Los Angeles County and its reputation as an innovator in crime fighting have grown in time.

Torrance City Marshals and Chiefs of Police:
Ben Olsen (1921)
Byron M. Anderson (1921–1924)
Loren F. Patterson (1924–1926)
Gerald M. Calder (1926–1938)
John H. Stroh (1938–1954)
Willard H. Haslam (1954–1956)
Percy G. Bennett (1956–1964)
Walter R. Koenig (1964–1970)
Donald E. Nash (1970–1991)
Joseph C. DeLadurantey (1991–1997)
James D. Herren (1997–2006)
John J. Neu (2006–present)

Completed on July 3, 1923, a combination firehouse, police station, and city hall was built at 1521 Cravens Avenue. The brick building housed city hall on the top floor while the police and fire departments shared the bottom floor. It included a one-room steel-lattice jail cage with four cells. Each cell had two steel bunks. A number of Torrance citizens objected to the location of this early police station. It was felt that the jail would never get much use. In those early years, rabid dogs, wandering children and livestock, occasional thefts of chicken, and the moral threat of a proposed pool hall occupied the Torrance policeman's mind.

One

THE EARLY YEARS
1921–1930

Ben Olsen, seen in this 1929 image, made a salary of $150 a month. The city later purchased him a badge and handcuffs at a total cost of $12.50. A concrete garage near the firehouse on the north side of Carson Street between Andreo and Cabrillo Avenues was rented for $2.50 a month, made habitable, and served as the first city jail for approximately two years.

On November 10, 1924, Loren F. Patterson, an investigator with the Los Angeles County District Attorney's Office, was appointed chief of the department and served in that capacity until May 1926. This image shows three of his men: Patrolman John Stroh (left), Patrolman "Shorty" Hamilton (center) and Sgt. J. B. Edwards. The early uniforms were green with brass "P" buttons.

Among other things, Chief Patterson and his police force continued rigidly enforcing Prohibition laws. This image from 1925 depicts the result of such a raid. From left to right are an unidentified Los Angeles County deputy sheriff, Patrolman William Phillips, Deputy Sheriff Charlie Taber, Patrolman Ira Young, Patrolman John Stroh, Desk Sergeant/Fireman Allen "Ollie" Stevenson, Sgt. J. B. Edwards, Chief Loren Patterson, Patrolman J. Brundrett, motorcycle officer Lester Stanley, and Patrolman "Shorty" Hamilton.

On May 5, 1926, Gerald M. Calder was unanimously appointed chief of police by the city of Torrance board of trustees, although he never aspired to it. Calder, who was known by thousands of his townspeople as "Jerry," was a successful businessman at the time of his appointment, having established an automobile repair shop in Torrance. He grew up in Reno, Nevada, and after running the gauntlet in a miner's life there, arrived in Torrance in April 1924. The eagle-topped badge had been introduced by this time.

In 1926, an adjacent site at 1523 Cravens Avenue was purchased, and a new two-story building was erected to house the fire department on the ground floor, with city hall occupying the second floor. The police department remained at the 1521 Cravens location and took over the entire building. This image shows the fire department/city hall in the front and the police department to the far right.

Motorcycle officer William "Bill" Malin was appointed by the Torrance Police Department in 1928 and became the third motorcycle officer in TPD's history (after Lester Stanley and Stanley Abbott). The "war against speedsters" soon became his primary responsibility. He is seen on his 1929 Indian Chief motorcycle in front of the police station on Cravens Avenue.

By 1929, the department had grown to 11 members. Seen from left to right are Patrolman A. L. Stuart, motorcycle officer William "Bill" Malin, Desk Sergeant/Fireman L. Paxton, Day Sergeant John Stroh, Chief Gerald "Jerry" Calder, Night Sergeant J. B. Edwards, Desk Sergeant/Fireman Allen "Ollie" Stevenson, Desk Sergeant/Fireman Jake "J. J." Benner, Patrolman Ben Olsen, Patrolman Frank Schumacher, and Patrolman George Dolton. The patrol vehicles are 1927 (left) and 1924 (right) Studebakers. The firemen pulled double duty.

Two

THE GREAT DEPRESSION YEARS
1930–1940

During the Great Depression, one of the annual events held in the city was a small-town tradition called the Factory Frolic. It was the sort of social event only a small town with great pride in its large factories would organize. Patrolman John Stroh is seen here in 1930 about to give the start shot to three of Torrance's beauties in a race at the event. One has to wonder how far they would get on those shoes.

Even though he had no prior law enforcement experience, Chief Calder served the city as chief of police for over 12 years until July 1, 1938, and then continued on as a police captain until April 1947. During this time, significant growth occurred in Torrance, resulting in police department personnel and equipment gradually being expanded. By August 1932, both of the department's patrol cars, a 1928 Studebaker and a 1930 Buick, had been overhauled and equipped with police radios. This image dates from 1933.

Also during the Great Depression years, a toy loan program was set up in which three stores in Torrance took part. Children's toys were displayed and could be checked out, similar to books in the library, for a period of up to one week. This image from 1932 shows Sgt. John Stroh with a young recipient who is obviously very happy with her choice. The uniform color had changed to dark blue by this time.

This image from 1933 shows the men who protected the life and property of 7,271 Torrance inhabitants in 18.88 square miles. From left to right are (first row) Sgt. J. B. Edwards, Sgt. John Stroh, Chief Gerald "Jerry" Calder, and city recorder and police judge C. T. Rippy; (second row) Patrolman Frank Schumacher, motorcycle officer William "Bill" Malin, Desk Sergeant/Fireman Jake "J. J." Benner, Patrolman Ernest "Ernie" Ashton, Desk Sergeant/Fireman John McMaster, Patrolman Everett Travoli, and Patrolman George Dolton.

This image from 1934 shows, from left to right, George Dolton, John Stroh, William "Bill" Malin, Ernest "Ernie" Ashton, J. B. Edwards, and Frank Schumacher. Note the decorations on Schumacher's chest. Bill Malin left the Torrance Police Department shortly thereafter and became a state traffic officer with the California Highway Patrol. He was tragically killed in the line of duty when a speeding motorist struck his motorcycle on July 4, 1940, after he was returning from an Independence Day assignment.

When Jake Stroh (left) traveled to Torrance in 1934 from his home in Greeley, Colorado, to celebrate his birthday with his twin brother, Sgt. John Stroh (right), they decided to pull a joke on Chief Calder. Jake donned one of John's uniforms and both appeared in front of the chief to startle him a bit and let him guess who was whom. Those little bow ties the men are wearing as part of their uniform were made out of leather.

Patrolman Percy Bennett, a Walteria resident, began his career with the Torrance Police Department on July 1, 1934. He was also a volunteer or "call man" for the Torrance Fire Department and helped build Fire Station No. 2, at 242nd Street and Neece Avenue. He is seen in 1934 with his young son, Mel, who himself would become a Torrance police officer exactly 20 years later, on August 3, 1954. Keeping the family tradition alive, Percy's granddaughter, Denise, joined the department as an officer on December 5, 1991.

In 1936, using federal relief funds, the city had several public buildings constructed. Since the old building at 1521 Cravens Avenue had started to deteriorate, a new police station and jail, as a wing of city hall, was constructed at 1519 Cravens. The police department moved to a temporary location at 1339 Post Avenue until the new facility was opened in July 1936. The modern neon sign above the door cost $89.45.

Positioned in front of the newly opened police building at 1519 Cravens Avenue in July 1936 are, from left to right, (first row) police judge Robert F. Lessing, motorcycle officer Ernest "Ernie" Ashton, Sgt. Frank Schumacher, Capt. John Stroh, Chief Gerald "Jerry" Calder, and Torrance mayor William H. Stanger; (second row) Patrolmen G. S. "Bill" Evans, Thomas Perkin, Fred Speheger, Percy Bennett, Willard "Pop" Haslam, Everett Travoli, and George Dolton. Note the diagonally worn leather straps attached to the Sam Browne belts used by eight of the officers.

This image from January 1938 shows, from left to right, (first row) motorcycle officer Ernest "Ernie" Ashton, Patrolman Everett Travoli, police judge Robert Lessing, Chief Gerald "Jerry" Calder, Mayor William Tolson, Patrolman G. S. "Bill" Evans, and motorcycle officer Percy Bennett; (second row) Patrolman Willard "Pop" Haslam, Patrolman Fred Speheger, Patrolman

Seen here in 1936 is patrolman Percy Bennett who, with Ernie Ashton, had become a motorcycle officer. The vehicle behind him is a 1936 Buick Model 41, which had been purchased for $328 plus the department's DeSoto as a trade-in.

Tom Perkin, Capt. John Stroh, Sgt. Frank Schumacher, Patrolman George Dolton, and Patrolman Curt Tolson. One current (Calder) and three future chiefs of the department (Stroh, Haslam, and Bennett) can be seen here.

A collage shows the personnel of the Torrance Police Department in 1938, after John Stroh assumed the title of police chief. Stroh, born in Lincoln, Nebraska, came to Torrance in 1924 from Loveland, Colorado, where he had lived most of his youth. He went to work for the Torrance Street Department running an asphalt roller for street superintendent William Gascoigne. Stroh remained with the street department until June 1924 and then went to work for the Pacific Electric shops, also in Torrance. On September 5, 1924, he was appointed to the police department as a patrolman.

On July 1, 1938, Capt. John R. Stroh was named director of public safety. Chief Calder was reduced to the rank of police captain, and fire chief Allen "Ollie" Stevenson was reduced to the rank of fire captain. Mayor Tolson felt that merging the two public safety departments under one head would increase efficiency and eliminate the necessity of adding three additional men to the fire department. This experiment ended after 11 months, with Stroh assuming the title of police chief and John McMaster being named fire chief.

Motorcycle officer Percy Bennett poses with his Harley-Davidson. Bennett was born outside London, England, in Harrow on the Hill before moving to Canada. He came to the United States in 1915 and resided in Burbank, San Pedro, and Torrance. He held jobs with the Yellow Taxi Cab Company and with the Coast Fishing Company in Wilmington before beginning his career with TPD as a patrolman on July 1, 1934. Before that, he had been the city's first dogcatcher as well as a paid volunteer or call man for the Torrance Fire Department.

Three

WORLD WAR II AND THE POSTWAR YEARS
1940–1950

This image from early 1940 shows Patrolmen Fred Speheger (left) and Willard Barnett in front of Harvel's Garage at 1618 Cravens Avenue. The patrol vehicle behind them is a 1938 Ford sedan.

This 1940 image shows Percy Bennett (left) and Chief Stroh inside the station. The facility was quite small, with a front desk, the chief's office, and a record-keeping area in the front. In the rear was the office of the desk sergeant, a radio room, and a small locker room. A jail with four individual male plus one female cell was located behind the desk sergeant's office. Arrestees were brought in through the side door, where there was a booking area.

Seen in 1940 is Capt. Frank Schumacher with the department's 1938 Ford. "Spike" had been a member of the U.S. Army's cavalry and had served on the Mexican border during World War I. He came to Torrance in 1920 and was one of the organizers of American Legion Bert S. Crossland Post No. 107. Crossland was the only Torrance resident killed in action during World War I. Schumacher joined the department as a patrolman on June 1, 1928, and was promoted to sergeant on May 1, 1934, and to captain on July 1, 1940. Health issues forced him to retire on July 1, 1951.

When Chief Stroh promoted motorcycle officer Percy Bennett to sergeant in July 1940, the chief gave Bennett's Harley-Davidson motorcycle to Patrolman Willard "Barney" Barnett, who thus became the sixth motorcycle officer in the department's history until he was involved in a head-on traffic collision one year later. Barnett survived and continued his career, but Chief Stroh had enough of police motorcycles and abolished them.

This image from 1940 shows the pistol range located near the water tower at 1001 Elm Avenue. This site was the primary shooting range for department personnel, along with a second public open-air range located behind the Walteria Businessmen Association office near what is now Rolling Hills Road and Hawthorne Boulevard. The former range on Elm Avenue was demolished when a new indoor range was built behind the station on Torrance Boulevard, and the site now belongs to the Torrance Municipal Water Department.

Patrolman Henry "Gene" Garner joined the Torrance Police Department on November 28, 1940. Like many, Gene enlisted in the U.S. Army during World War II, earning the rank of sergeant. He is seen here (left) along with Barney Barnett (right) in front of Barney's residence at 2007 Andreo Avenue in 1941. Barney's Harley can be seen parked in the background. Before joining TPD, Garner had been a sparring partner for boxer Joe Louis. Upon his return from military service, he was appointed acting sergeant on May 11, 1943. He left the department in July 1945 to join the California State Police Department.

This 1941 image shows Sgt. Percy Bennett (left) and Patrolman Tom Perkin (right) in front of the station. The patrol car is the 1938 Ford, and Percy's Harley-Davidson motorcycle, now assigned to Barney Barnett, can be seen on the left. A spare room inside the adjoining city hall at 1511 Cravens Avenue was used for some court cases, but most were held in the Redondo Beach Municipal Court.

On July 6, 1941, Officer Willard Barnett was involved in an on-duty traffic collision when his motorcycle struck a car at the intersection of Torrance Boulevard and Valencia Street (later renamed Earl Street). Barnett was responding to a grass fire when the accident occurred, was thrown off his motorcycle, and suffered a fractured left wrist and bruises. He was taken to Torrance Hospital, where he recovered from his injuries. TPD subsequently had no police motorcycles for 12 years, until Chief Haslam created a new motorcycle detail consisting of Patrolmen William "Bob" Lewis and Dave Cook in 1954.

This 1942 image depicts Chief Stroh in his office. Torrance mayor William H. Stanger had appointed him to the rank of sergeant in 1929. After receiving a high grade from the Torrance Civil Service Commission in a competitive examination for police captain, Stroh was advanced to that rank in 1934. At the time of his appointment to chief, Stroh was married and had two children. Both would later join their father as members of the Torrance Police Department, Lucille as an acting desk sergeant, police matron–file clerk, and policewoman, and Jay as a patrolman.

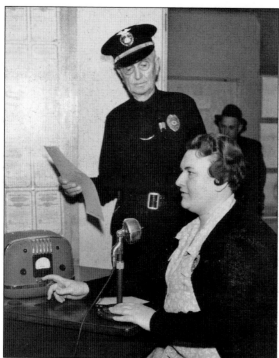

Lucille "Lucy" Stroh, the daughter of Chief Stroh, was appointed acting desk sergeant for the Torrance Police Department on October 20, 1942. She is seen operating the two-way radio with Capt. Jerry Calder at the station's dispatch console. Her father can be seen in the background. Lucy also served as police matron and file clerk, and on August 1, 1950, was appointed policewoman. Lucy left TPD on May 1, 1951, in order to pursue a career with the Compton Police Department as a policewoman.

This 1943 image depicts Los Angeles-based U.S. Navy Shore Patrol Headquarters Unit. Four Torrance police officers were assigned to this unit during World War II. Three of them can be seen in this photograph: Percy Bennett (sixth from the left, fifth from the top), Willard "Barney" Barnett (third from the left, seventh from the top), and Karl Friberg (second from the left, top row). The fourth member of the unit, Adrian Thornberry, was not present when this photograph was taken.

Another image of U.S. Navy Shore Patrol Headquarters Unit taken in 1944 shows two Torrance Police Department members in the performance of their duties for the U.S. Navy. From left to right are shore patrolmen Karl Friberg and Barney Barnett (both TPD). Shore patrolmen ? Penhallow and ? Jones round out the quartet at the Union Railroad Depot in downtown L.A., where they provided protection for a young Northern European princess.

This image from 1944 depicts Chief Stroh (right) with radio and movie actress Jane Withers, a popular child actress of the 1930s, and the unidentified chief of the another Los Angeles County police department during an appearance at radio station KGER. During World War II, Withers performed in more than 100 bond and camp tours within the United States and sent her extensive collection of 3,500 dolls, most received as gifts from her fans, on tour to raise money for the war effort.

This October 5, 1945, image shows, from left to right, Judge Otto Willett, U.S. Army Air Corps captain Louis Zamperini, and Chief Stroh. Zamperini had arrived home to a hero's welcome after spending two and a half years in Japanese prison camps during World War II. He was well known by TPD during his teenage years while growing up in the city. Zamperini wound up representing his country in the 1936 Olympics before becoming an Army Air Corps bombardier in B-24 Liberators.

This image from January 1946 taken in El Prado Park depicts TPD's returning World War II veterans. From left to right are the following: (first row) Larry Benton (U.S. Navy), Swayne Johnson (U.S. Navy), unidentified (U.S. Army), and Roy Sullivan (U.S. Army); (second row) Adrian Thornberry (U.S. Navy), Patrolman D. C. "Carmel" Cook (not a veteran), Curt Tolson (U.S. Navy), and Sgt. Percy Bennett (U.S. Navy).

By January 1946, all of TPD's World War II veterans had returned home. Seen in this image is the U.S. Navy contingent back in police uniform. From left to right are (first row) Karl Friberg, Sgt. Percy Bennett, and Curt Tolson; (second row) Willard "Barney" Barnett, Swayne Johnson, and Adrian Thornberry. Of note is that Friberg is still wearing the LAPD-style uniform hat, while the others are all wearing the new eight-point hats. Friberg, Johnson, and Tolson are all wearing whistle chains with the whistle outside the pocket, and Barnett is still wearing the small leather bow tie.

In 1946, a lunch party was held at Vurp's Café and Cocktail Lounge, 1434 Marcelina Avenue, for several TPD veterans who had returned home from the war. From left to right are Roy Sullivan (U.S. Army), unidentified (U.S. Army), Capt. Jerry Calder, Barney Barnett (U.S. Navy), George Dolton, Swayne Johnson (U.S. Navy), Capt. Ernie Ashton, Larry Benton (U.S. Navy), Pop Haslam, Chief Stroh, Sgt. Percy Bennett (U.S. Navy), Sgt. Bill Evans, Karl Friberg (U.S. Navy), Curt Tolson (U.S. Navy), Alex "Porky" Thompson, and Capt. Frank Schumacher.

This image from January 1947 shows TPD personnel inside city council chambers after having received formal instruction from the FBI. From left to right are Sgt. Percy Bennett, Capt. Frank Schumacher, Leonard "Tex" Beal, Capt. Ernest "Ernie" Ashton, Douglas "Carmel" Cook, Karl Friberg, Adrian Thornberry, an unidentified FBI agent, Alex "Porky" Thompson, an unidentified

By 1946, Patrolman Thomas H. Perkin (right) had left the Torrance Police Department for the Escondido Police Department in San Diego County, where he would become police chief. He is seen here in Escondido's uniform along with his former colleague, TPD's Bill Evans. The strength of the Torrance Police Department had increased to 16 policemen at this time.

FBI agent, Willard "Barney" Barnett, Chief John Stroh, John Maestri, Mervyn "Hank" Porter, an unidentified FBI agent, Larry Benton, an unidentified FBI agent, Sgt. G. S. "Bill" Evans, retired chief Gerald "Jerry" Calder, Jess Holmes, and Swayne Johnson.

Chief John Stroh can be seen in this 1946 image at the FBI building in Washington, D.C. The chief was the first Torrance police officer to attend and successfully complete the 12-week FBI National Academy, which he did from April 8 to June 28, 1946. The academy, then held in Washington, D.C. (now in Quantico, Virginia), furnishes a broad general course of police training to experienced police officers for the purposes of helping them perform official functions as police instructors and police executives.

On September 24, 1946, the department received permission to purchase a new Ford and trade in their 1942 DeSoto. Patrolman Douglas "Carmel" Cook is seen here with the pride of the fleet, the 1946 Ford black-and-white.

This 1948 image shows Patrolmen Bob Wright (left) and Douglas "Carmel" Cook at the rear of the station on Cravens Avenue. Carmel or "D.C." Cook was appointed to the department on March 8, 1946, while Bob Wright was hired on February 1, 1948. Both men would have long careers with TPD (Cook 26-plus years and Wright 31-plus years), and both would attain the rank of lieutenant.

On July 12, 1948, city council approved the expenditure of $1,112.98 for the department to purchase a three-wheeled motorcycle for parking enforcement. In this 1948 image, Patrolman John Maestri is seen with the Harley-Davidson three-wheeler along with a passenger seated on the back. City clerk Albert Bartlett (left) and Chief Stroh can be seen behind the bike. The Grand Theater at 1522 Cravens Avenue and the Sports Club Café at 1528 Cravens Avenue can be seen in the background.

Pictured is life as it was at TPD in 1948 for, from left to right, Patrolmen Don Nash, D. L. Clark, John Maestri (pouring coffee), Jesse Holmes, and Sgt. Percy Bennett. They are enjoying "code-7," or mealtime. A foot beat in the downtown area was a routine assignment for these patrolmen. A flagpole at Sartori and Cabrillo Avenues was equipped with a red light on top of it. This was the primary means of communications with the station on Cravens Avenue. When the red light was illuminated, the patrolmen on foot beat knew they had to get to a telephone near the base of the pole and call the station for an assignment.

In 1948, the city of Torrance boasted a population of around 8,000 inhabitants. Seen during that year is Patrolman Leonard "Tex" Beal with the Harley three-wheeler at the rear of the station at 1519 Cravens Avenue. Of note is Officer Beal's cross-draw holster on his Sam Browne belt, as well as the shoulder emblems on his uniform shirt. This was TPD's first shoulder emblem, or patch, and it consisted of the California golden bear in between the words "Torrance Police" in dark blue on a white background.

On June 12, 1949, Swayne Johnson crossed home plate after hitting a grand-slam home run. For a number of years, Swayne was the playing manager for TPD's baseball team and the motivating force behind the promotion of Sunday baseball in Torrance. Swayne started his career with TPD on August 12, 1941. After an approximate three-year military leave of absence during World War II, he again reported for active duty in 1952 during the Korean War. At TPD, he was promoted to sergeant on February 8, 1949, and to lieutenant on April 1, 1954. After 29 years of service, he retired on August 1, 1970.

Four

LAW ENFORCEMENT IN THE "ALL-AMERICA CITY" 1950–1960

Seen in March 1951 is the entire department. From left to right are (first row) Capt. Willard "Pop" Haslam, city attorney Jim Hall, Sgt. Alex "Porky" Thompson, Sgt. G. S. "Bill" Evans, Chief John Stroh, Sgt. Karl Friberg, Sgt. Percy Bennett, Capt. Ernest "Ernie" Ashton, and Capt. Frank Schumacher; (second row) matron/file clerk Lucille Stroh, matron/file clerk Carol Wright, Al Jackson, Hyman "Mickey" Fischer, Jim Thompson, Harvey Turrentine, Douglas "Carmel" Cook, Don Hamilton, and Larry Benton; (third row) Ralph Walker, Gale Whitacre, Jesse Holmes, Nolan "Robbie" Robinson, Ted Morris, John Maestri, Myles Hamilton, and William "Bob" Lewis; (fourth row) Joe Miles, Don Nash, Bill Mitchell, Harold "Zeke" Trezise, Mervyn "Hank" Porter, Al Winkler, and Gus Rethwisch. Ashton and Bennett were the department's first detectives.

Patrolman Bob Wright was called into active duty with the U.S. Army in the summer of 1950 and was sent to Korea. Shortly before this, his friends from the department held a party for him at Higgins Brickyard on 182nd Street. Clockwise from the left front are Joe Miles, Pat Miles, Sydney Maestri, Bernice Holmes, John Maestri, Bob Wright, Carol Wright, Esther Cook, Betty Thompson, Jim Thompson, Ruby Rethwisch, and Gus Rethwisch.

Chief Stroh's son, Jay, was hired by the Torrance Police Department as a patrolman on May 16, 1951. He left TPD to join the Los Angeles County Sheriff's Department a year later, where he rose to the rank of acting captain. He became chief of police in El Segundo from 1966 until 1971 and in Inglewood from 1971 until 1982. After spending a year as director of corporate security at Hollywood Park, he was appointed director of the California Department of Alcoholic Beverage Control by Gov. George Deukmejian in 1983 and again by Gov. Pete Wilson in 1991. He retired on July 15, 2000, which brought to a close 49 years as a public servant.

Patrolman Dave Cook was hired by TPD on January 18, 1952. He is seen here in a 1952 image investigating his very first traffic collision at the intersection of Torrance Boulevard and Cota Avenue.

Chief Stroh resigned on January 31, 1954, eight months short of serving the city for 30 years. A retirement reception for him was held at the Downtown Torrance Lions Club. Among all his other attributes and accomplishments, Chief Stroh is noted for having instituted the first formalized approach to police training at the Torrance Police Department. As a result, new patrolmen were sent to a two-week training school in Los Angeles administered by personnel from the FBI.

Taken at Chief Stroh's retirement reception, this image shows, from left to right, Sgt. G. S. "Bill" Evans, Chief Stroh, Torrance city manager George Stevens, Los Angeles County sheriff Eugene W. Biscailuz, and Torrance city councilman Nickolas "Nick" Drale.

During the chief's retirement reception, a delegation from his department presented him with a retirement gift. It seems the chief liked working with wood. From left to right are Alexander "Porky" Thompson, Don Nash, Dave Cook, Bob Wright, Bill Mitchell, and Chief Stroh.

Assistant Chief Willard H. Haslam was appointed the new chief of police of the department on February 9, 1954. "Pop," as he was known, started his career with the Torrance Police Department on May 13, 1935, as a patrolman. He soon attained the rank of sergeant and was promoted to captain on February 8, 1949, and to assistant chief on April 21, 1952. Among other things, Chief Haslam ordered the reinstitution of a motorcycle squad equipped with Harley-Davidsons.

This image from early 1954 shows the TPD patrol fleet at 1519 Cravens Avenue. From left to right are Patrolman Jack Hahn, Patrolman Douglas "Carmel" Cook, Patrolman Jim Thompson, Patrolman Don Hartel, Patrolman Archie "Al" Jackson, Chief Willard "Pop" Haslam, Patrolman Larry Benton, and Patrolman Bill Crow. The vehicles are 1953 and 1954 Chevrolets.

After 13 years of absence, TPD's motorcycle squad was resurrected by Chief Haslam on October 1, 1954. Seen here from left to right are Sgt. G. S. "Bill" Evans, William "Bob" Lewis, Chief Haslam, and Dave Cook. They would be joined by a third motorcycle officer, Al Jackson, effective September 1, 1955. Cook and Lewis owned these motorcycles and leased them to the city for traffic enforcement for $80 per month. This would continue until September 2, 1958, when three new Harley-Davidson motorcycles were purchased by the city.

This 1955 image shows motorcycle officer Cook investigating a traffic collision on the Torrance side of the intersection of Western Avenue and 234th Street. The wheel and arrow traffic enforcement insignia can be seen underneath his shoulder emblem. Note the eight-point hat he is wearing with the obligatory sunglasses. Helmets were not yet worn and/or were not mandatory at this time. Dave is using his Harley as his office and had found a place for his flashlight and his department-issued baton on his bike.

In 1956, both city hall and the police department moved to modern locations in the 3100 block of Torrance Boulevard as part of a new civic center complex. The police station at 3131 Torrance Boulevard was dedicated on August 11, 1956, and consisted of 9,317 square feet of much-needed space. Also in the mid-1950s, the South Bay Court was relocated to 3231 Torrance Boulevard (the current City of Torrance Human Resources Department) before a new facility was built at 825 Maple Avenue.

This image, taken right before the official opening of the new station in August 1956, shows, from left to right, the following: (first row) Chief Willard "Pop" Haslam, Assistant Chief Percy Bennett, Wally Nitz, Hyman "Mickey" Fischer, Jim Davis, Kenny Halbert, Charlie Oates, file clerk and matron Charlene Alarcon, Hughy "Buck" Ingram, and Gus Rethwisch; (second row) Jack Hahn, Lt. Mervyn "Hank" Porter, Bob Hammond, Frank Solis, Gerry Snyder, Ralph Bezanson, and Al Jackson. Note that patrol officers had switched to a new shoulder emblem, still with the golden bear in the center but now with Torrance Police in gold letters on a blue background. Traffic officers continued to wear the original emblem.

This 1956 image shows Torrance mayor Albert Isen (center) presenting a certificate of appointment to Maxine Hahn (right) upon her becoming a Torrance policewoman. The mayor's secretary can be seen on the left. The taking of a promotional civil service examination for policewoman had become mandatory by this time. Maxine, the only woman on the force having graduated from El Camino College with a degree in police science, was hired by TPD as a police matron–file clerk in 1953.

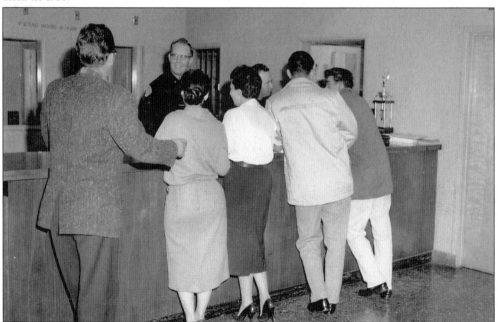

This 1956 image shows Bob Wright (left) and Jack Hahn conducting everyday business at the station's front desk.

After only three years at the helm, Chief Haslam resigned in March 1957, and Assistant Chief Percy Bennett was appointed acting chief of police. A retirement reception for Chief Haslam was held shortly afterwards. This image, taken during that reception, shows, from left to right, Mabel Haslam, Chief Haslam, Acting Chief Percy Bennett (at the microphone), and his wife, Addie.

At the same reception, Torrance mayor Albert Isen is seen pinning Chief Haslam's retirement badge on him. Mabel Haslam is seen at the left, and Acting Chief Percy Bennett at the right.

Assistant Chief Percy Bennett was officially appointed chief of police on October 1, 1957. After starting his career with TPD in 1934, Percy was promoted to sergeant in July 1940 and worked as a supervisor in patrol before and after his tour of duty in the U.S. Navy during World War II. In March 1947, Chief Stroh selected him as one of Torrance's first detectives (Ernie Ashton was the other one) to start a new division. On July 1, 1955, he was promoted to assistant chief of police.

In this image from November 11, 1957, patrol watch commander Lt. Alexander "Porky" Thompson is caught taking a power nap at his desk during the morning shift.

Seen in a December 1957 image during a Christmas party are, from left to right, the following: (first row) Kenny Halbert, Jim Kirby, Jim Daniel, Frank Sotis, Charlie Oates, Dorothy Volmerding-Culverhouse, Russ Culverhouse, Ralph Bezanson, Edward "Glyn" Boyce, Charlene Alarcon-Winkler, Mel Bennett, Lt. Gus Rethwisch, retired Chief Pop Haslam, and Lt. Swayne Johnson; (second row) Vince Davey, Bruce Bishop, Frank Solis, Bob Hammond, unidentified, Sgt. Bill Mitchell, Myles Hamilton, Don Lemaster, Sgt. Hughy "Buck" Ingram, Maxine Hahn, Jack Hahn, Chief Percy Bennett, Regina Ryan, Bernice Florence, Evelyn Stanford, Alice Speheger, Lt. Karl Friberg, and Sgt. Donnie Hamilton; (third row) Jim Foster, Jim Davis, Wally Nitz, Tom Wooldridge, Bob Daly, Gerry Snyder, Paul Findley, Ralph Walker, Al Winkler, Al Jackson, Lt. Joe Miles, Sgt. Bob Wright, Don Hartel, William "Bob" Lewis, Sgt. Bill Winther, Lt. Alex "Porky" Thompson, Tom Pattishall, and Sam Piazza.

Seen here in late 1957 is one of the Torrance Police Department's first graduation photographs at the Los Angeles County Sheriff's Academy. From left to right are Patrolman Douglas Nice, Patrolman Richard "Dick" Humphrey, Sheriff Eugene Biscailuz, Assistant Chief Mervyn "Hank" Porter, Undersheriff Peter J. Pitchess, Patrolman Robert Jones, Patrolman Arthur "Ray" Fuller, and Patrolman Robert Such.

This 1957 image shows Chief Percy Bennett with TPD's traffic division personnel; from left to right are (first row) Chief Bennett and Patrolmen Don Lemaster, Charlie Oates, Sam Piazza, Don Hartel, and Bill Mitchell; (second row) motorcycle officers William "Bob" Lewis, Archie "Al" Jackson, and Dave Cook, Patrolmen Myles Hamilton, Tom Pattishall, and Ray Silagy, and Sgt. Joe Miles. The traffic officers are wearing white eight-point hats, and most have the "winged wheel" traffic enforcement insignia below their shoulder emblem. Of note also is that all except the three motorcycle officers and Bill Mitchell are still wearing the shoulder patches with the California golden bear on blue background.

This 1958 image shows motorcycle officer Archie "Al" Jackson on his 1952 Harley-Davidson Glide Pan Head bike in front of the station. He is wearing the half-shell helmet that became standard issue. Note the leather military flap-style holster for his department-issued revolver as well as the four road flares carried on the right side of the Harley adjacent to the rear wheel. Jackson joined TPD on September 11, 1950, and was appointed motorcycle officer on September 1, 1955. Like Lewis and Cook, he owned the motorcycle and leased it to the city until September 1958.

In this 1958 image, a traffic accident at the intersection of Hawthorne Boulevard and Sepulveda Boulevard is being investigated and traffic control is being provided. In the background on the northeast corner, a sign can be seen announcing plans to build the Del Amo Center, a 35-acre regional shopping center, at that location.

In this image dated January 20, 1959, Torrance mayor Albert Isen (left) and Chief Percy Bennett (right) can be seen presenting Patrolman Gerald "Jerry" Snyder (second from the left) and motorcycle officer Tom Wooldridge (third from the left) with copies of a city council resolution commending them for their actions above and beyond the call of duty at the scene of an automobile accident.

Chief Bennett is seen in April 1959 in front of the station with TPD and other agency personnel who have attended and completed an FBI-sponsored fingerprint school at the Long Beach Police Academy. TPD personnel are, from left to right, the following: (first row) Patrolman Harry Owens (striped shirt), Patrolman Hughy "Buck" Ingram, Patrolman Donnie Cook, Chief Percy Bennett, Policewoman Maxine Hahn, FBI agent and instructor Bill Stout, and two unidentified. The second row includes Sgt. Bob Hammond (second from left) and Patrolman Doug Nice (far right).

Having some fun in the sun on July 25, 1959, is motorcycle sergeant William "Bob" Lewis. The motor officers started wearing helmets for added protection by this time. Sadly this measure would not be enough to protect Sergeant Lewis only one month later.

This 1959 image shows the intersection of Sepulveda Boulevard and Hickory Avenue looking west. This was the scene of a traffic collision investigated by Torrance Police Department traffic division personnel. Note the skid marks in the eastbound lane and the wooden oil derricks in the field on the north side of Sepulveda Boulevard.

The Torrance Police Department has managed the school crossing guard program since June 1944, when one guard was assigned to Walteria Elementary School. Crossing guards are civilian employees whose responsibility it is to assist Torrance's elementary school children in safely crossing the streets at school crossings in congested areas. This 1959 image shows one of those 19 dedicated crossing guards in the performance of her duties on Artesia Boulevard.

The Torrance Police Officers Association, in conjunction with professional promoters, had been holding annual police variety shows since 1938. Seen here at the front desk in 1959 is policewoman Maxine Hahn (second from left) holding show tickets in her hand while promoter Dick George (far right) signs the contract for the 22nd annual benefit show and dance. Looking on are Sgt. Bob Hammond (left), Patrolman Richard "Tiny" Thompson (rear), and Patrolman Albert "Al" Winkler (right).

Tragedy struck the Torrance Police Department on Sunday, August 23, 1959, when motorcycle sergeant William "Bob" Lewis was killed in the line of duty. Sergeant Lewis, while riding his police motorcycle and attempting to stop a traffic violator, was struck by a vehicle in the intersection of Hawthorne Boulevard and Carson Street. At the time, this was an uncontrolled intersection without traffic signals. Sergeant Lewis, a 10-year veteran of the force, was born in Seattle, Washington, and was appointed patrolman on October 3, 1949. He became a motorcycle officer in October 1954.

The funeral service for Sergeant Lewis was held on Thursday, August 27, 1959, at 2:00 p.m. at Halverson-Leavell Mortuary at 1223 Cravens Avenue. A total of 102 motorcycle officers from Los Angeles County agencies as well as the California Highway Patrol attended the service.

This overhead image of the funeral service for Sergeant Lewis shows Torrance Police Department and other law enforcement personnel lined up at Halverson-Leavell Mortuary to pay their last respects. Prior to the commencement of the service, TPD personnel had assembled at the former city hall parking lot at 1511 Cravens Avenue, from where they marched in formation to the mortuary.

A long procession of police motorcycles, as well as a vehicle motorcade, escorted Sergeant Lewis to his final resting place at Green Hills Memorial Park at 27501 South Western Avenue in San Pedro. This image shows the interment ceremony as Sergeant Lewis is laid to rest by pallbearers from the Torrance Police Department and the California Highway Patrol.

This image from December 1959 shows the uniform division's morning shift at parade rest. From left to right are (first row) Lt. Joe Miles, Sgt. Ralph Walker, and Patrolmen Harry Owens, Charlie Oates, Bob Lydon, Lee Graber, unidentified, and Ray Ouellette; (second row) Patrolmen Bill Crow, Bob Stone, Jim Doyle, Bob Jones, unidentified, Harry Pelley, and ? Scheibeler.

Also pictured in December 1959, the uniform division's day shift personnel are, from left to right, Lt. Bob Wright, Sgt. Jack Hahn, Patrolmen Richard "Tiny" Thompson, Ray Silagy, Paul Singleton, Harry Waugaman, Bob Dunn, and Fred Jackman.

Seen in this December 1959 image is the uniformed division's afternoon shift with, from left to right, (first row) Patrolmen Jim Popp, Frank Solis, Joe Capriotti, Ron Nicolai, Vince Davey, Bob Such, Jim Bell, and Tom Pattishall; (second row) Jim Fowler, Gene Bailleul, Dan Murray, Mort Hesse, Bob Daly, Doug Nice, Paul Lembke, Al Winkler, Sgt. Bill Mitchell, and Lt. Alex "Porky" Thompson.

Lined up in this December 1959 image is the traffic division with, from left to right, the following: (first row) Lt. Don Nash, motorcycle sergeant Dave Cook, motorcycle officers Ken Halbert, Tom Wooldridge, Bruce Bishop, Dick Humphrey, Jim Kirby, and Don Lemaster, and matron–file clerks Dorothy Peters, Carol Craig, and Pat Speaks; (second row) Darrell Lanham, Edward "Glyn" Boyce, Tom Lloyd, Ralph Bezanson, Eugene Gillette, Clifford Smith, Gerald "Gerry" Snyder, Arthur "Ray" Fuller, Tom Arnold, Don Hartel, Tom Patishall, and Bill Winther.

TPD's detective bureau personnel in December 1959 are, from left to right, (first row) Detective Eugene "Gene" Erbetta, matron–file clerk Dorothy Volmerding, policewoman Maxine Hahn, Detective Jim Davis, Detective Sam Piazza, matron–file clerk Charlene Alarcon, and Sgt. Don Hamilton; (second row) Sgt. Hyman "Mickey" Fischer, Detective Donnie Cook, Detective Wally Nitz, Detective Lee Ashman, Detective Myles Hamilton, and Detective Lonnie Brown.

TPD had its own pistol team, which entered competitions throughout the state. Seen in this December 1959 photograph at the outdoor range on Elm Avenue are, from left to right, Patrolman Bob Jones, Sgt. Bill Mitchell, Sgt. Jack Hahn, Patrolman Gene Erbetta, and Sgt. Dave Cook.

Among the new equipment, a model 52A mobile radar unit was placed in service in 1959. Patrolman Don Hartel (third from left) explains the unit to members of the Torrance Civitan Club, a service organization devoted to improving the lives of children and adults with developmental disabilities. Capt. John Maestri of the department's uniform division stands to the far right.

This image, also from 1959, shows Patrolman Don Hartel, then assigned to the traffic division, putting the first radar car to good use. The unit scientifically recorded the speed of a traffic offender. It was also used in determining safe speeds in order for speed limits to be reduced or increased for safe traffic flow.

Five

REORGANIZATION
1960–1970

Chief Bennett, an avid horse rider, is seen in this 1960 image on his Palomino Golden Glory. The chief was an active member of the Torrance Mounted Police, and whenever time would permit during the year, he would saddle up his horse to participate in a variety of parades throughout Southern California.

Seen in 1961 are personnel assigned to the records and identification division with their division commander. From left to right are matron–file clerks Evelyn Stanford, Patricia "Pat" Hall, Wanda Madden, and Bernice Florence, Lt. Douglas 'Carmel' Cook, and matron–file clerks Donna Kerns, Lois Reynolds, and Margaret "Kitzie" Virden.

In this image from May 21, 1961, Patrolman Julian "Paul" Lembke is seen wearing a newly installed seat belt in one of the department's marked black-and-whites. Safety equipment such as shown here was installed in the entire TPD fleet.

Seen in December 1961 are Lt. Swayne Johnson as Santa Claus (right) with Patrolman Richard "Tiny" Thompson bearing Christmas gifts while paying a visit to a young patient at a local Torrance hospital.

In 1962, the department was still using the public pistol range located near what is now Rolling Hills Road and Hawthorne Boulevard. Department range master Lt. Alex "Porky" Thompson is seen using a 2-inch, .38-caliber revolver on that range. Note that patrol division officers had, by this year, switched back to the original white shoulder emblem.

This image from February 1963 shows members of TPD's motorcycle squad after taking delivery of seven new Harley-Davidson police motorcycles from Southwest Harley-Davidson at 1853 West Carson Street in Torrance. From left to right are motorcycle officers Clifford Smith, Don Lemaster, Ralph Bezanson, Ken Halbert, Bruce Bishop, Dick Humphrey, Tom Wooldridge, and Jim Kirby, Chief Percy Bennett, Capt. John Maestri, Lt. Don Nash, motorcycle sergeant Dave Cook, and Harley-Davidson dealer Bob Reagan.

In 1963, the Torrance City Council designated May 12 to May 18 Police Week and May 14 Peace Officer Memorial Day. This image from May 14, 1963, shows, from left to right, Torrance councilman Nick Drale, councilman Ken Miller, Mayor Albert Isen, Los Angeles County supervisor Kenneth Hahn, Chief Bennett, and city manager Wade Peebles at the police memorial service conducted in front of city hall.

Lt. Swayne Johnson and Patrolman Don Hartel can be seen in this 1963 image in the station's briefing room. Note the small kitchen in the background.

This image from February 13, 1964, shows the patrol division's morning shift standing at attention in front of the station. Seen from left to right are (first row) Patrolmen Larry Robinson, Don Morrison, Ted Goudy, Charlie Oates, Kevin Eliason, John Frontado, Fred Jackman, and Jim Farrar; (second row) Patrolmen Jim Fowler, Ray Schneider, Richard "Tiny" Thompson, John Ainsworth, Jim Doyle, Julian "Paul" Lembke, Charles "Chuck" Bloom, and Ray Gros. Helmets were mandatory for patrolmen at this time.

Also seen in February 1964 are personnel assigned to the juvenile division. From left to right are (first row) Detectives Ray Silagy, Margaret "Peggy" Duval, and Jim Daniel; (second row) Detectives Archie "Al" Jackson, Dick Schwanbeck, Phil Joseph, and Clifford Smith.

When Chief Bennett resigned in early 1964, the search for a new chief resulted in the appointment of Walter R. Koenig, a 25-year Los Angeles Police Department veteran and captain of its Hollenbeck Division, effective on July 6, 1964. For the first time in almost 40 years, a police chief had been appointed from outside the ranks of TPD. During his term, Chief Koenig influenced many positive and noteworthy accomplishments, resulting in the Torrance Police Department being recognized as among the finest in the nation. Significant growth in personnel resources, expansion of the police facility, a complete reorganization, and total importance placed on police training were among his accomplishments.

This image from July 26, 1964 shows TPD's pistol team at the Fourth Annual Law Enforcement Pistol Championship, held in Stockton, California. From left to right are (kneeling) Patrolmen Bob Armstrong and Don Henry; (standing) Patrolman Edward "Glyn" Boyce, Sgt. Dave Cook, and Patrolman Noel Cobbs.

In December 1964, Chief Koenig (center) promoted matron and file clerk Margaret "Kitzie" Virden to policewoman and Officer Jim Daniel to sergeant. Daniel was a nine-year veteran of the department who had worked assignments in patrol, juvenile, and traffic. He was also a graduate of the University of Southern California's Delinquency Control Institute. Virden joined TPD in 1959 after nearly a year of service with the Newport Beach Police Department.

Seen at their January 1, 1965, promotion ceremony are Sgt. Bruce Bishop and Policewoman Margaret "Peggy" Duval. Bishop was appointed as a patrolman to the department on September 1, 1956, while Duval joined TPD as a police matron and file clerk on November 14, 1960. She became the city's fifth policewoman after successfully passing the civil service exam for that position.

Rioting erupted at midnight between striking and non-striking workers at the Harvey Aluminum Company at 19200 South Western Avenue on Wednesday July 31, 1965. The plant was located in Los Angeles; however, the employee parking lot was located across the street within the jurisdiction of the City of Torrance. An unidentified man can be seen here grabbing hold of the baton of a Torrance policeman as other TPD personnel come to his aid.

Chief Koenig (left) with the Annual Youth Safety Run winners at the Dick Allen Rambler car dealership. Members of police-sponsored car clubs would vie throughout the year for a chance to participate in the Annual Youth Safety Run, a contest showing that teenage drivers could drive safely as well as economically. Some of the car clubs sponsored by the TPD were The Pharaoh's Pacers, "T" Timers of Torrance, The Performers, The Three Castlemen, and The Assyians.

Taken at the Lakewood Country Club, this 1965 image shows, from left to right, TPD policemen John Frontado, Jim Randall, Ernie Smith, and Jim "Homer" Davis participating in the South Bay Peace Officers golf tournament.

"The story you are about to see is true. The names have been changed to protect the innocent," says a voice at the beggining of the television show *Dragnet*. *Dragnet* actor and producer Jack Webb, famous for portraying Los Angeles Police sergeant Joe Friday on radio and television, is seen in this August 1965 image with TPD's Dave Cook after the latter's promotion to lieutenant.

In the early 1960s, the rapid growth of both the city and the police department led to the latter quickly outgrowing the original police building. On September 21, 1965, ground was broken to expand the station from 9,317 to 30,425 square feet. Seen here at that formal ceremony are, from left to right, Torrance councilman Jay Beasley, Chief Walter Koenig, councilman Ken Miller, and Mayor Albert Isen.

Seen here on November 15, 1965, are the beginnings of a full basement that would be part of the addition of 21,108 square feet of working space on the west side of the police facility. The basement would include, among other things, a new briefing room, officers' report-writing room, communications center, photography lab, locker facilities, and a break area.

This image shows the graduation of Los Angeles Sheriff's Department Academy Class 108 on December 10, 1965. From left to right are (first row) Keith "Kit" Mason, Chief Walter Koenig, Pat Findley, Lois Reynolds, and Sheriff Peter J. Pitchess; (second row) Richard "Dick" Augenstein, Herman "Bear" Garleb, Gary Hilton, Don Gross, and Dan Bush. All eight officers successfully completed 16 weeks of academy training at Biscailuz Center in East Los Angeles. Whistle chains running from the right shoulder epaulette to the shirt pocket were a mandatory part of the uniform.

A May 1966 image shows joint crowd control training in progress in the civic center complex by members of TPD's special enforcement detail and the Los Angeles County Marshal Office's emergency enforcement detail. Both departments had entered into a mutual-aid pact to combine forces in the event of riots and other emergency situations.

The Torrance City Council proclaimed May 15 to May 21, 1966 Police Week and Wednesday, May 18, Peace Officers Memorial Day. On that day, Chief Koenig, Torrance mayor Albert Isen, and city councilman George Vico conducted a formal inspection of department personnel. The ceremony afterwards honored TPD sergeant Bob Lewis, who lost his life in the line of duty in 1959. Honored guests were former Torrance police officers Carel "Dutch" van Wankum (in wheelchair), Leo Gonzales (behind van Wankum), and Ron Nicolai (not pictured), all retired because of serious injuries suffered in the line of duty.

Seen on Saturday, May 21, 1966, is motorcycle officer Ernie Smith in the station's compound along with other officers getting ready for the annual Armed Forces Day parade. The house trailer seen on the left was used to hold shift briefings. The white structure in the back is the indoor pistol/shooting range.

Also seen getting ready for the Armed Forces Day parade in this May 21, 1966, image are, from left to right, Assistant Chief Mervyn "Hank" Porter, Officer Ted Goudy, and Chief Walter Koenig.

This 1966 image shows construction of the first floor moving along. This area would house the detective and records divisions, the watch commander, and an expanded jail. When the police station was originally built in 1956, TPD's manpower stood at 60 people. By 1965, this had tripled to a work force of 187 personnel. Seen in the background, the construction of the South Bay courthouse at 825 Maple Avenue was taking place at the same time.

Seen investigating a grand theft auto incident on July 29, 1966, in a Torrance Sav Co Market parking lot is Sgt. Paul Nowatka.

In 1966, the ABC television series *Batman* (January 1966 to March 1968) came to Torrance. In this image taken during a break in filming at Torrance Beach, TPD policemen Richard "Dick" Schwanbeck (left) and Larry Robinson can be seen checking out the inside of the famous Batmobile.

Seen here is an artist's conception of the $335,950 addition to the police facility at 3131 Torrance Boulevard. The official dedication of the new annex took place on Wednesday, September 7, 1966. An open house and guided tours of the building followed the ceremony.

On September 7, 1966, after the dedication of the police building expansion, Chief Koenig requested that the previous chiefs of the department sign and present certificates of appointment to members of the department hired during their respective administrations. Seen in this image are, from left to right, former chief John Stroh (1938–1954), former chief Willard Haslam (1954–1957), former chief Percy Bennett (1957–1964), and Chief Walter Koenig.

Sometimes four minds are better than one! This 1966 image shows, from left to right, patrol division sergeants Bob Such, Ray Silagy, Wally Nitz, and Harry Waugaman trying to figure things out.

Shown here in a November 2, 1966, publicity shot are (from left to right) TPD motorcycle officer Dan Murray, H. Ted Olsen, Lt. Bob Wright, actor Lee Anthony, and motorcycle officer Gene Guest. The occasion was the annual Boy Scout dinner.

This February 1967 image shows Officer Jim Weyant (left) and Sgt. Mel Hone, both of whom were selected to take part in the Torrance-Alameda police exchange program. The unique pilot program was conceived as a result of meetings at the 1966 conference of the International Association of Chiefs of Police in Philadelphia and further developed at the police chiefs section of the League of California Cities in San Diego by Chief William Tulloh of Alameda and Chief Walter Koenig of Torrance.

On February 5, 1967, Chief Koenig can be seen giving Sergeant Hone (left) and Officer Weyant their send-off to Alameda. The interdepartmental police exchange program, scheduled between February 5 and February 22, 1967, was the first of its kind. Its purpose was to bring to two California police departments a broader outlook and an opportunity for learning from each other.

In this image, (from left to right) Torrance Police Department sergeant Mel Hone and officer Jim Weyant greet their counterparts, Alameda Police Department officer Bob Carlson and sergeant Joe Totorica. Both departments exchanged two officers and a marked patrol car. After arriving at their host city, each officer was given a regular patrol assignment as a partner of a uniformed officer of the host city and worked a variety of assignments, including accident investigation and traffic enforcement.

Seen in this 1968 image in front of the police station are Torrance officers Mike Dersham (far left) and Jim Bell (far right) with two visiting bobbies from Great Britain. The term "bobby" refers to Sir Robert Peel, the police reformist of the Metropolitan London Police in 1829.

The Torrance Police Department tragically lost their second officer when David Seibert was killed in the line of duty on Thursday, August 10, 1967. Officer Seibert had responded to a silent robbery alarm at the Foods Company Market at 17500 Crenshaw Boulevard at 8:45 in the morning. Unbeknownst to him, a robbery by an escaped convict was taking place inside the store. Officer Seibert was shot three times by the suspect when he entered the market. The suspect fled the location but was captured near Salt Lake City, Utah, two weeks later. On February 22, 1968, a jury found him guilty of the first-degree murder of Officer Seibert.

Torrance Police personnel converge at the Foods Company Market at Crenshaw Boulevard and Artesia Boulevard, the scene where TPD officer David Seibert was fatally shot during a robbery on August 10, 1967. Officer Seibert, a two-year veteran, was born in Richmond, California, and spent his teenage years in Kernville, California. He was hired by the Torrance Police Department on April 1, 1965, at 23 years of age, after serving as an apprentice-trainee, the forerunner of the police cadet program. (*Daily Breeze* photograph.)

Officer Seibert's funeral service took place on Monday, August 14, 1967, at Gamby Mortuary, 25001 Narbonne Avenue, in the city of Lomita. In this image taken after the service, Dr. Frank Rischelieu, pastor of the Torrance Church of Religious Science, who officiated the service, precedes TPD pallbearers Lt. Hyman "Mickey" Fischer and Officers Ron Bryning, Herman Garleb, Mike Riley, Don Flaherty, and Tom Handsaker from the chapel. (*Daily Breeze* photograph.)

The procession was escorted by over 50 police motorcycles to Inglewood Park Cemetery, 720 East Florence Avenue, in the city of Inglewood for graveyard services and interment. This image shows the Torrance Police Department honor guard. From left to right, Officers Greg Fahnestock, Gary Meyer, Brad Parsons, and Larry Caudell render last honors by firing a three-volley gun salute. (*Daily Breeze* photograph.)

Taken on August 14, 1968, during the patrol division's afternoon watch briefing in the basement of the station, this image shows, from left to right, (first row) John Senger and Gary Hilton. Also included are Bruce Bott, Barbara Orton, Nolan Dane, Mike Draeger, Clayne Virgin, Paul Reuter, Wally Murker, Vic Grijalva, Erv Palica, Rollo Green, dispatcher Karen Adams, Dave Hancock, dispatcher Audrey Landreth, Hugh Ashley, and Ed Finn.

This image from September 1968 shows, from left to right, Officer Ray Schneider, Sears Del Amo manager Herm Link, Sgt. Bob Such, and police chief Walter Koenig. Sponsored by Sears and Roebuck, both officers received appointments to attend Class 47 of the University of Southern California's Delinquency Control Institute, a 12-week educational program designed to combat juvenile crime. Operating continually since 1946, the institute is the only program of its kind.

Detective Gary Rippstein was shot by an auto theft suspect on Saturday, December 21, 1968. Detective Rippstein and Detective Bob Holmes were attempting to arrest the suspect at his wife's apartment in the 600 block of Eighth Street in the city of Hermosa Beach. The detectives were fired upon by the suspect as soon as they entered the bedroom, and Detective Rippstein was struck. Detective Holmes and responding Hermosa Beach officers returned fire and killed the suspect. Detective Rippstein was taken to South Bay District Hospital in Redondo Beach, where he succumbed from his gunshot wound on Sunday, December 22, 1968.

This image shows Chief Koenig (far left) and other TPD and allied agency personnel lined up and awaiting to enter the Church of Jesus Christ of Latter-Day Saints at 4110 West 226th Street in Torrance on Friday, December 27, 1968, for the funeral service. Officer Rippstein, a six-and-a-half-year veteran of the department, was born in Downey, California, and graduated from Torrance High School. He was hired by the Torrance Police Department in April 1962. An ordained minister, Rippstein was appointed by Chief Koenig to the newly created position of police chaplain, the agency's first, in 1965. (*Daily Breeze* photograph.)

In this image of the casket being escorted from the church are, from left to right, Lt. Bob Wright (blue uniform), unidentified funeral director (glasses), and Capt. Don Nash. Pallbearers include Officer Harold Maestri, Officer Bob Holmes, Sgt. Jim Weyant, Officer Don Flaherty, and Officer Lee Turner. Sgt. Bob Armstrong (right, foreground) would later play taps at the interment. (*Daily Breeze* photograph.)

Almost 1,000 people, including more than 300 police officers, paid final tribute to Detective Rippstein. At the conclusion of the church service, the procession was escorted to Green Hills Memorial Park at 27501 South Western Avenue in San Pedro for interment services. This image, taken at Green Hills, shows members of the Torrance Police Department honor guard (far left) rendering honors for Detective Gary Rippstein by firing a three-volley salute as other members of the detail stand at attention (far right). (*Daily Breeze* photograph.)

This 1968 image shows the Torrance Police Officers Association–sponsored police basketball team with, from left to right, Officers Keith "Kit" Mason, Don Morrison, Sgt. Jim Daniel, Officers Erv Palica and Dave Marsden, and Cadet Bob Kammerer.

This image, taken in April 1969, shows the Torrance Police Department honor guard; from left to right, Sgt. Bob Armstrong and Officers Wally Murker, Ron Traber, John Senger, and Rick DeSpain escort Avon Koenig, the wife of Chief Koenig, as well as an unidentified bagpipe player at the Hollywood Palladium in Los Angeles for the annual TPD variety show.

The Armed Forces Day Parade, a Torrance tradition, originated in 1960, when Mayor Albert Isen, with the help of the Torrance Chamber of Commerce, organized the first parade as a tribute to friends and fellow Americans who had served in the armed forces. Held every year since that date, Torrance's parade has the distinction of being the longest-running military parade sponsored by any city in the nation. This image, taken on May 17, 1969, shows grand marshal and five-star general Omar Bradley awaiting the start of the parade.

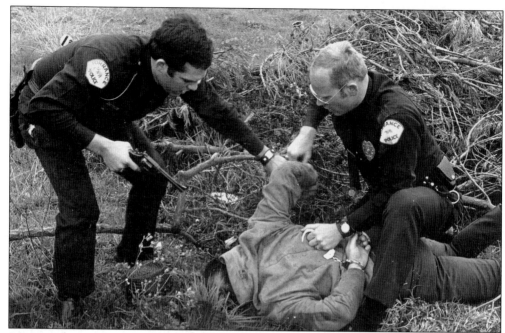

Seen here on January 19, 1970, Officers Peter Herley (left) and Don Gross (right) are taking a "suspect" into custody during a tactical training exercise dubbed Barricaded Felony Suspects, which took place at some abandoned buildings next to the Torrance Municipal Airport. Pete Herley joined TPD in 1966 as a student trainee. He became a regular officer on June 6, 1967, and eventually received promotions to sergeant and lieutenant. On June 7, 1987, he was appointed chief of police of the Tiburon Police Department in Marin County in the San Francisco Bay Area. He retired from Tiburon in 2001 after spending 35 years in law enforcement.

TPD's narcotics section is pictured in front of their office, known as the "back room." Shown in this 1970 image are, from left to right, Alan Marshall (California Bureau of Narcotics Enforcement), Detective Nolan Dane, Sgt. Jim Weyant, Detective Jim Ferguson, Detective Jim Griffith, and Detective Dave Marsden.

Six

STABILITY AND GROWTH
1970–1980

On February 4, 1970, after having served several months as interim chief, Capt. Donald E. Nash was appointed chief of the Torrance Police Department. Chief Nash began his career with the department as a patrolman on October 25, 1948. Having served for over 20 years, risen through the ranks, and studied the approaches and management philosophies of four chiefs prior to his appointment, Chief Nash was well-qualified to assume the top executive role of a modern police department in an active city.

Former TPD officer Willard "Barney" Barnett had left the department in June 1947 to join the California Highway Patrol. While with the CHP, he was selected and served as official driver for California governors Edmund G. "Pat" Brown (1959–1967) and Ronald Reagan (1967–1975). Barnett retired on March 1, 1973, after a 35-year career in law enforcement. He is seen in this 1973 image with Governor Reagan.

This image from 1974 shows patrol division lieutenants Jim Foster (left) and Jim Randall in the rear compound of the station about to conduct a watch inspection of, from left to right, Officers Dave Hancock, Steve Ross, Joe Simpson, Keith Rush, Julian "Paul" Lembke, Clayne Virgin, Al Rhoads, Mike Browne, and Chuck Hrehor.

Seen in this 1974 image is patrol officer Vic Grijalva. His vehicle was a very fast 1971 Plymouth Satellite. Note the red roof-mounted rotator, commonly referred to as a gumball machine, the "alley lights" on both sides, and the public-address speaker in front.

Policewoman Penelope "Penny" Koenig became TPD's first female police officer on May 16, 1974, after passing a physical agility test and meeting certain other criteria. She was originally hired as a policewoman on July 7, 1969. As a police officer, she became immediately eligible for fieldwork and was therefore transferred to the patrol division. Before that time, policewomen were limited to working inside the station, where they answered telephones, processed female prisoners, and/or worked the front desk. This 1974 publicity photograph shows her placing Officer Don Hartel, posing as a suspect, in the back of her patrol car. Of note are the uniform skirt and shoes.

In March 1974, the Torrance Police Department started issuing portable cassette tape recorders and several tapes to its patrol officers. The recorders were used to tape crime reports during the shift, as is seen being done by Officer Jim Ulrich in this October 1975 image. They were then turned in to a records clerk, who would transcribe it into report form. This would allow the officer to remain both visible and in the field.

Every recruit who has ever entered the police academy will relate to this image. Seen in November 1975, Torrance cadet Raul Ramirez is receiving some one-on-one attention from his Los Angeles County Sheriff Department drill instructor on the first day of the academy.

At the conclusion of the 1965–1966 expansion of the station, the dispatch center or "radio room" was housed in the basement. This image from 1975 shows Officer Penny Koenig at one of the two dispatch consoles. Note the large map of the city with the various unit designators and the "on the air" sign on the wall in the background. Incoming calls were written down on IBM cards by the complaint-taking officers, time-stamped, and handed to the communications operators, who would dispatch the call. The wood paneling on the wall was later replaced by a large mural depicting a mountain scene.

In this 1976 image of the radio room, Officer Mike Paolozzi can be seen at the "Officer in charge" (OIC) position. On the other side of the glass to his left are the positions of the complaint-taking officers. Torrance PD, unlike many other agencies, used—and still uses—sworn police officers as complaint takers. They are the public's first line of contact when calling the department.

Seen on Friday May 14, 1976, are, from left to right, Sgt. Dennis Frandsen, Officer Kit Mason, Officer Denny Cook, and Lt. Gerry Snyder as they get ready for the formal department inspection by Chief Nash during Police Week.

This image from the same day shows Chief Nash (left) and Lt. Don Feil (background) inspecting, from left to right, Officers Ralph Blount (partially obscured), Wally Murker, Danny Williams, Jim Ulrich, Jerry Wallace, Ron Ruby, Jim Ferguson, and Lee McCoy, all in class-A uniform with eight-point hats. The chief is wearing an Eisenhower, or "Ike," jacket.

Chief Nash (back to the camera) gives some personal attention to Officer Jim Davis (hired four years after the chief on September 16, 1952) during the Police Week observance formal inspection. Also shown in this May 14, 1976, image are Torrance mayor Ken Miller (back to the camera, far left), Officer John Spindler (left), motorcycle officer Paul Hulst (right), and Lt. Bob Armstrong (foreground, far right).

After the formal inspection, a memorial ceremony for TPD's three fallen officers was held inside the Torrance City Council chambers. Seen in this May 15, 1976, image, Military Order of the Purple Heart medals were awarded to Officers Dave Williams (left) and Tom Jarvis (right) by the Veterans of Foreign Wars. Both officers were wounded by a robber during a holdup of the Southwood Cleaners at 22232 Palos Verdes Boulevard on Thursday, November 6, 1975. Jarvis was shot twice in the back and Williams's right arm was shattered above the elbow by a single gunshot. Despite his injuries and before collapsing, Officer Jarvis managed to fire one round, which struck the suspect and led to his capture a block away.

Torrance Police Department's first Special Weapons and Tactics (SWAT) team was created in 1975 and consisted of two units made up of a sergeant, a sniper, and four entry officers. SWAT teams are designed to provide expertise in tactics and weaponry during hazardous and life-threatening situations such as barricaded suspects, hostage situations, and high-risk warrant service. This image from 1979, taken at basic SWAT school taught by the FBI at Hamilton Air Force Base in San Rafael, California, shows, from left to right, (top row) TPD officers Charles McCullough, Pete Snodgrass, Steve Gilliam, Leon Darley, and Dave Hancock (far right).

On Monday December 3, 1979, at 6:00 p.m., an explosion ripped through several 800,000-gallon gasoline storage tanks at the Mobil Oil refinery at 3700 West 190th Street. The explosion, followed by a second one at 1:00 a.m. Tuesday morning and the resulting massive fire, led to the evacuation of about 200 people along Del Amo Boulevard and the closure by TPD of several streets surrounding the refinery. From left to right in this image, taken on December 4, 1979, Officers George Morales, Jim "Perch" Chamberlain, and Jim Ulrich can be seen receiving coffee from American Red Cross personnel during a rest break.

Seven

A NEW FACILITY
1980–1990

This image from 1980, taken during a traffic division briefing in the basement briefing room of the station, shows motorcycle officer Mike Quinn (left) and motorcycle sergeant Ron Brumbelow. Note the classroom desk chairs and the board on the wall behind them that contains mug shots, or photographs and identifying information of known criminal offenders.

Seen here on that same 1980 day in front of Torrance City Hall, are from left to right, motorcycle officers Mike Quinn, Steve Ross, and Mark Sims and their riding sergeant, Ron Brumbelow. Note that Quinn, Ross, and Sims are still wearing the old-style half-shell helmets, while Brumbelow has already transitioned to the new three-quarter-shell helmet, which offers better protection. The bikes are Harley-Davidson Sportsters, smaller and lighter than the other Harley models.

At the time of this photograph, the police station on Torrance Boulevard still possessed an old-fashioned telephone switchboard with plugs located on the first floor off the records division and across from the watch commander's office. Seen in this 1980 image is communications operator Kathy Diaz assigned to switchboard duty during her shift.

In 1980, Torrance Police Department range masters Jim "Homer" Davis and Dave Frawley developed a new weapons training program. Unlike the regular monthly qualification shoot, the new decision-making program conducted at the department's indoor range was conducted in semi-darkness, with movable targets and with loud sound effects. Homer Davis is seen running and monitoring the program in his range office in this March 1981 image. (*Daily Breeze* photograph.)

In this image from October 1980, LASD drill instructor Robert Ouellette is seen making his point to Torrance cadet Marsha Barnet at a formal inspection during week 10 of the 16-week Los Angeles County Sheriff's Academy in East Los Angeles.

This 1981 image shows construction under way on the present police facility at 3300 Civic Center Drive. At a cost of $8.3 million, the three-story building was designed with an open work-area concept, having a minimum number of bearing walls so that future modifications could be made with minimum expense and disruption. Included in the 74,000-square-foot building are a modern, well-appointed jail and an emergency operations center capable of meeting the public safety needs of the city for emergencies and crisis situations.

This image shows the last briefing (day watch) held at 3131 Torrance Boulevard in March 1982, prior to the move to the new facility. Shown from left to right are (first row) watch commander Lt. Larry Robinson and Sgt. Paul Besse; (second row) Officers Rich Connor, Larry Ely, and Paul Hill; (third row) Officers Rick Allen and Tom Winchester, (fourth row) Officers Mark Wittenberg and Tim Hillis.

The first briefing in the new facility (afternoon watch) took place on that same day in March 1982. Seen in this image are, from left to right, (first row) Officers Steve Hanks and Tim Treher; (second row) Officers Ed Webb, Jim Carreras, and Sterling Tanouye; (third row) Officers Jim Ulrich and Phil D'Addario; (fourth row) Officers Brent Scott and Dave Bry. The new Torrance police building was formally dedicated on February 26, 1982.

Seen here in 1982 is the morning watch. From left to right are the following: (first row) Bill Ferrell, Rick Glass, Ed LaLonde, Sgt. Mike Hertica, Dick Augenstein, Pedro "Pete" Velis, Maury Dandoy, and Mark McDermott; (second row) Lt. Jim Papst, Jim Ulrich, Charles "Chuck" Bloom, Bob Bowman, John Prins, Charles McCullough, Vern "Mike" Alexander, and Andy Conahan.

This 1982 image shows day watch personnel. From left to right are the following: (first row) Sgt. Sue Rhilinger, Kevin Berman, Sterling Tanouye, Steve Unglaub, Steve Bock, Penny Koenig, and George Daley; (second row) Lt. Jim Foster, Tim Hillis, Dave Crespin, Jeff Meyer, Karl Young, and Lester "Kim" Fronk.

This 1982 image shows the afternoon watch. From left to right are the following: (first row) Rich Connor, Tom Jarvis, Dave Blunt, Lt. Ray Silagy, Robin Kakumu, and Manuel "Henry" Lopez; (second row) Ron Pobuda, Rick Allen, Gary Meyer, Lyndal "Sprad" Spradlin, John Sibley, Larry Ely, and Sgt. Chuck Hrehor; (third row) Sgt. Rollo Green, Rich Silagy, Leon Darley, Dave Dick, John Senger, and Kurt Barton.

Field training officers (FTO) are experienced officers who provide continual training and evaluation of probationary officers after graduation from the police academy. Seen in this 1982 image are FTO committee members, from left to right, (first row) Steve Harvey, Steve Hovsepian, Jack McDonald, Sgt. Paul Besse, and Tom Dempsey; (second row) Jim Ulrich, Dave Hancock, Gary Meyer, Jerry Wallace, Clayne Virgin, Rich Silagy, and Lt. Larry Robinson; (third row) Sgt. Roy Beaver, Sgt. Sue Rhilinger, Phil D'Addario, Mike Tamble, Ed LaLonde, Andy Conahan, Bill Ferrell, and Ed Estrada.

Another image from 1982 shows the motorcycle detail. From left to right are Officers Tom Handsaker, Tom McDaniel, Dick Humphrey, Steve Ross, Bob Leinweber, Richard "Andy" Anderson, and Steve Monson, Sgt. Noel Cobbs, and Officer Dennis Lefevre. Out of this group emerged two police captains (Ross and Leinweber).

In this 1982 image, the driver of a Volkswagen convertible has come to an unorthodox stop on Sepulveda Boulevard at Orange Street. Observing the scene while waiting for a tow truck are, from left to right, Officers Steve Bock, Gary Webb, and John Senger.

On October 10, 1974, a group of citizens met to discuss the idea of a South Bay Medal of Valor Award for police and firefighters. From that meeting, the South Bay Medal of Valor Award Committee has grown to include all nine mutual-aid cities of the South Bay. The first Medal of Valor Awards luncheon was held on March 20, 1975, attended by all nine cities and eight chambers of commerce in the South Bay. This 1982 image shows Chief Nash (first row, fifth from left) with Torrance Police Department medal recipient Officer Bill Ferrell (second row, sixth from left).

This image from 1983 shows the detective bay and forgery detail detectives Jack Latham (left background) and Ed Estrada. In 1983, the division consisted of a crimes persons section (robbery, homicide, criminal assault, sex crimes, and forgery), a crimes property section (theft, burglary, auto theft, bunco/fraud, warrants, and tactical alarms), and a juvenile section (area investigators, special investigations, youth services, diversion, and the explorers post).

Seen in this 1983 image are, from left to right, shopping center (or mall) detail officers Bob Bowman, Mike "Vern" Alexander, Pedro "Pete" Velis and Al Rhoads on the top floor of the J.C. Penney parking structure at the Del Amo Fashion Center. The shopping center program provides specialized enforcement as well as service to the shop owners in the city's major shopping centers. There has been a Torrance Police Community Center (sub-station) at Del Amo Fashion Center since 1987.

In this image taken during the May 21, 1983, police memorial ceremony inspection, the reviewing party, from left to right, includes Mayor Jim Armstrong (suit), Capt. Jim Weyant (partially obscured), and Chief Don Nash. Nash is directing his attention to Jack, a five-year-old German shepherd from Denmark, and his handler, Officer Bob Kammerer (standing next to Jack).

In this image, Chief Don Nash (front, center) and Mayor Jim Armstrong (suit) can be seen continuing their inspection. Also seen included in the photograph are Officers Ron Peterson, Mike Terry, Steve Gilliam, Ron Ruby, and John MacKinnon. On the far left, Sgt. Mike Hertica can be seen standing at attention.

In 1983, the beach patrol detail consisted of Officers Andy Conahan (left) and Dave Hancock (right). They are seen in front of the old Dodge Tradesman black-and-white prisoner transport van. The intent of the beach patrol program is to provide consistent and specialized patrol during the summer months along Torrance's 1.5-mile-long beachfront.

In 1979, research was conducted and a proposal submitted by Officer Bob Kammerer to start a canine detail within the Torrance Police Department. The proposal gained approval and resulted in the purchase of four dogs and the training of their handlers. TPD's K-9 teams began working the streets in February 1981. This image from 1983, taken during a recertification course in Riverside, shows, from left to right, Bob Kammerer and Jack, John Sibley and Fax, Frans Breitsamer of the Bavarian (German) State Police K-9 School, Dave Reaver (Adlerhorst Kennels), Dick Augenstein and Nicki, and Tom Jarvis and Artos. Mike Majors, one of the four original Torrance handlers, had left the department for the Boise, Idaho, Police Department with his dog, Astor.

Shown in front of the police facility in 1984 are Lt. Dave Marsden (left) and Sgt. Jim Wallace (right). Jim Wallace had been with TPD since April 1961 and Dave Marsden since September 1964.

In this 1984 image from a SWAT training day, team members Ed LaLonde (left) and Dennis Addington can be seen scouting a tactical problem. Of note is the Israeli-made Uzi 9-mm that Addington is carrying, at the time a standard-issue SWAT weapon for TPD.

This image taken during the 1984 Armed Forces Day parade shows motorcycle officers Steve Bock (left) and Dave Smith on their Kawasaki 1000 police motorcycles in front of a California National Guard M-60 tank of the 40th Infantry Division (Mechanized), based in Los Alamitos. In 1984, the motorcycle detail transitioned from Harley-Davidson Sportsters to Kawasakis.

In 1984, the department obtained two three-wheeled all-terrain vehicles for use at Torrance Beach during the summer season. Officer Walt Delsigne is seen with one of them. Officers assigned to the beach patrol detail wear short-sleeved polo shirts and dark blue shorts. The three-quarter shell helmet did not become mandatory wear.

Each year the department holds a crime prevention fair at the Del Amo Fashion Center. Booths, displays, and demonstrations are presented to familiarize the public with its police department and to offer tips on crime prevention. In this 1984 image, services officer Rosie Neprud is seen presenting McGruff, the crime dog known for teaching kids how to be safe and healthy.

A detective's job never stops. Seen hard at work on their caseload in this 1984 image are auto theft detectives Leonard Thorpe (left) and Dave Hancock. There were no personal computers at the time of this photograph.

Officer Tom Keller was shot and killed on Thursday, April 17, 1986, after responding to an armed robbery call in the downtown area. Unbeknownst to officers, the suspect, upon entering the Torrance Sport Shop at 1421 Marcelina Avenue, had armed himself with an M-1 carbine rifle. After responding officers arrived on scene, the suspect opened fire from inside, fatally striking Officer Keller. Eventually an entry was made into the store by TPD's SWAT team, and the suspect was found dead from a self-inflicted gunshot wound.

Officer Keller's funeral service took place on Tuesday, April 23, 1986, at St. Rafael's Catholic Church, 5444 Hollister Avenue, in the city of Santa Barbara. A long procession was then escorted to the Calvary Cemetery at 199 North Hope Avenue in Santa Barbara, where more than 500 uniformed officers attended the graveside service. In this image, pallbearers, including Torrance officers John Blair (center left) and Doug Duckson (center right), carry the flag-draped coffin of Tom Keller onto the cemetery grounds. (*Daily Breeze* photograph.)

The tradition of bagpipes played at police department funerals in the United States goes back over 150 years. The pipes have come to be a distinguishing feature of a fallen hero's funeral. This image shows the lone piper who played "Amazing Grace" at the graveside ceremony for Officer Keller.

A tree was planted in Tom Keller's honor on the lawn in front of the Torrance police facility. This image shows the TPD personnel who took part in this ceremony. Officer Tom Keller had joined the Torrance Police Department on April 26, 1982, and had previously served with the U.S. Marine Corps, and as an Explorer Scout and reserve deputy sheriff with the Santa Barbara County Sheriff's Department.

Seen here in 1986 is communications operator Debbie Rogers at dispatch console 1. She is still using IBM cards, sent to her via a conveyor belt by the complaint-taking officers in the back, to dispatch calls.

In this image from 1986, Officer Dave Frawley is seen answering an incoming call from the public for assistance. He sits at one of the two consoles directly behind the communications operators. Seen to his left is the conveyer-belt system.

Torrance police officer Jim Mock is seen in this 1986 image transferring latent lifts he obtained at a crime scene onto a lift card. Jim Mock was a member of TPD's crime scene investigation (CSI) detail for many years and instrumental in the further development of the unit. The CSI detail within TPD's patrol bureau was started in 1971. Its main task is the collection and preservation of physical evidence. Each of the officers assigned to the unit have been specially trained as field evidence technicians to handle photography, fingerprints, castings, and so forth.

The second generation of police canines had entered service with the Torrance Police Department by 1984. From left to right are Dave Crespin with Condor, Ron Pobuda with Ikarus, John Prins with Wodan, and John Senger with Birko in this 1986 image.

Detective division personnel assembled in 1986 on the grassy knoll are, from left to right, the following: (first row) secretary Irene Alvarez, Howard Frazier, secretary Lyn Uvaney, Kit Mason, Leonard Thorpe, Lt. Lee Turner, Sgt. Jack McDonald, Sgt. Mike Hertica, secretary Fran Bollinger, juvenile diversion counselor Dianne Pales, and Gary Hilton; (second row) Ed Estrada, Ron Ruby, Bob Leinweber, Jeff Lancaster, Jim Cook, Gary Meyer, Steve Boutwell, Larry Fuller, and Sgt. Ron Ingram; (third row) Tom Nancarrow, Dave Nemeth, Mike Browne, Marc Wilkins, Don Sherwood, and Dennis Lefevre; (fourth row) Steve Monson, Joe Martin, Barry Walsh, Jim Lorentz, George Morales, and Joe Simpson.

Seen in this 1986 image are records division personnel, from left to right, (first row) Sue Powell, Linda Phelan, Beatrice Carbonnel, Adela Ewert, Naomi Wright, and Cecelia Valenzuela; (second row) Edie Miller, Estelle Marcopoulos, Peggy Denning, Alberta Bell, and records manager Bernice Osborne; (third row) Janet Weaver, Margie Oliver, Shirley Green, Audrey Escobar, Kathy Tynen, and Clyde McClure.

Torrance Police Department crossing guard Hazel Kenney was struck by an automobile and killed while performing her duties protecting the children of Torrance in the crosswalk of Palos Verdes Boulevard and Ruby Street on December 17, 1986. She was the mother of TPD officer John Sibley. Funeral services took place at St. Andrew's Presbyterian Church, 301 Avenue D in Redondo Beach. This image shows the procession of Torrance black-and-whites departing the church for the graveside services.

Graveside services for Hazel Kenney were held at Pacific Crest Cemetery, 2701 West 182nd Street in Redondo Beach. Visible in this image, besides many of Hazel's fellow crossing guards, are (from left to right) TPD pallbearers Dale Robbins, Sgt. Rollo Green, Karl Young, and Lt. Dennis Frandsen, as well as Bob Kammerer (partially obscured), Larry Davis, and Jim Carreras.

Also seen in 1986 is range master Larry Fuller inside his domain. Continuous training is essential to the effective operation of the police department. The range master coordinates all weapons training and conducts regularly scheduled qualification programs for all sworn personnel.

In this 1989 image, Officer Bob Bowman and his bike are having no problem attracting attention during a "show and tell" at one of the local elementary schools.

The Baker-to-Vegas Challenge Cup Relay is the largest law enforcement foot race in the world. It is a 120-mile, 20-stage relay race beginning in Baker, California, and finishing in Las Vegas, Nevada. The first race was held in 1985, and the Torrance Police Department has had a team in every race since 1987. This image shows the 1988 team, from left to right: (first row) Steve Hovsepian, Steve Bock, Jim Cook, Ed Lalonde, Gary Hilton, and TFD dispatcher Chris Maag; (second row) Jim Weyant, Tom Handsaker, Leonard Thorpe, Dianne Pales, Jim Mock, Tom Dempsey, and Scott Margolin; (third row) Noel Cobbs, Al Trumble, Glen Mosley, Jim Papst, Dave Hancock, and Jeff Lancaster.

During 1987, a band called Beyond the Law was formed by several TPD members. The band performed at several functions, such as DARE graduations, downtown festivals, the Taste of the South Bay, Torrance Police Officers Association Christmas parties, and others. They also performed the national anthem at Los Angeles Lakers games. Seen from left to right are Beyond the Law members Dave Dick, Bill Dorman, Greg Satterfield, Jim Wallace, and Scott Margolin.

Eight

EXCELLENCE THROUGH TEAMWORK
1990–2006

Culminating 42 years of distinguished service in law enforcement, Chief Nash's last day of work was May 13, 1991. The longest tenured chief in the history of the department, Don Nash served 21 years in that capacity. This 1991 image shows the chief with his final command staff; from left to right are (first row) Capt. Jim Weyant, Capt. Nolan Dane, and Capt. Larry Robinson; (second row) Capt. Jim Randall, Chief Don Nash, and Deputy Chief Jim Popp.

During the chief's retirement luncheon, held on March 13, 1992, former TPD lieutenant Swayne Johnson was one of the guests. He is seen here (right) with his longtime friend Don Nash.

Effective December 1, 1991, Joseph C. DeLadurantey, a former Los Angeles Police Department captain, took the helm of the Torrance Police Department. Chief DeLadurantey embraced community-oriented policing and a problem-solving philosophy. This led to three significant additions to the department: the community lead officer (CLO) detail and the citizen volunteer and the partners in policing (PIP) programs.

Fingerprint evidence collected from the scene of a crime is commonly instrumental in obtaining convictions. In this 1991 image, CSI officers Dave Koenig (left) and Henry Lopez attempt to obtain workable lifts from a Colt .45 semi-automatic pistol that was used in a crime.

Seen in 1991 is the patrol morning watch, which is still commonly known as the graveyard watch. From left to right are (first row) Mike Wilmoth, Larry Mitchell, Phil Gallegos, John Blair, and Chris Kozak; (second row) Sgt. Lyndal "Sprad" Spradlin, Larry Hardin, Dave Petersen, Tom Dorsey, John To, and Lt. Harold Maestri.

Also seen in 1991 is the patrol day watch. From left to right are (first row) Lt. Dennis Frandsen, Henry Lopez, Jeff Haire, Mike Tokle, Brett Andersen, and Ron Ruby; (second row) Al Trumble, Sean Papst, Marc Wilkins, Terry Tokle, Sgt. Gary Webb, and Sgt. Danny Williams.

Last but not least is the patrol afternoon watch. From left to right are the following: (first row) Sgt. Scott Margolin, Bob Picker, Jeff Woods, Al Tucker, Andy Conahan, and Juan Delvalle; (second row) Steve Andrews, Mike Wheeler, Chester Pitts, Bob Bowman, Bruce Bott, Kevin Taualii, Marty Dempsey, and Steve D'Anjou.

This 1991 image shows motorcycle officer Richard "Andy" Anderson at a combined Torrance Police Department–Redondo Beach Police Department driving-under-the-influence (DVI) checkpoint on Sepulveda Boulevard east of Palos Verdes Boulevard.

This 1991 image shows longtime City of Torrance motorcycle mechanic Rick Warren (seated on the Kawasaki) with, from left to right, Sgt. Tim Hillis, Steve Burke, Steve Harvey, Steve Hanks, Derek Powell, Bill Dorman, Richard Anderson, Glen Mosley, and Leon Darley.

Sponsored by the Torrance Police Officers Association (TPOA), the Santa Float, a Torrance tradition, first appeared on the city's streets in the weeks preceding Christmas 1967. The float, pulled by a truck, escorted by police cars, and preceded by a vehicle equipped with loudspeakers, makes its rounds through the city during the weeks before Christmas, stopping on residential streets where Santa, TPOA members, and their families hand out candy canes and dispense good cheer to all. This 1989 image shows the first float along with Officers Mike Wheeler (left) and Rich Connor.

The first float lasted 25 years before literally falling apart from wear and tear in 1992. That year, plans for a new 40-foot-long sleigh were drawn out on a napkin at Hof's Hut restaurant. From left to right, longtime lead vehicle driver Henry Schmidling, Sgt. Lyndal Spradlin, and Officer Mike Wheeler are seen putting Santa's seat on the new sleigh, still under construction.

During 1992 and 1993, this core of officers—(from left to right) Steve Ross, Mike Terry, Steve Badenoch, Tim Hillis, and Lyndal "Sprad" Spradlin (Mike Wheeler was not present when this photograph was taken)—used their off-duty time to build the new float from scratch in an empty warehouse. The cherry-red float has Rudolph and all his reindeer friends onboard, strings of lights, garlands, a white picket fence, a chimney that blows smoke and, of course, Santa's seat.

Even a burglary of the warehouse and a theft and vandalism of the sleigh's sound equipment, tires, rims, and seat cushions during November 1993 could not stop Santa from making his customary rounds that Christmas. Cash donations from officers, civilian employees of the department, residents, and businesses poured in so that the float could be repaired in time to hit the streets.

DARE stands for Drug Abuse Resistance Education. The curriculum is taught to sixth-grade students during the course of a semester by a uniformed police officer. Seen in 1993 are, from left to right, DARE officer Jim Carreras, Chief DeLadurantey, Sgt. Dave Smith, and DARE officer Jim Ulrich with the department's DARE van, a 1991 Chevrolet Lumina.

On parade day, the prologue check-in area is usually a beehive of activity, with parade entries reporting in up to the last minute prior to the 1:30 p.m. start. In this May 20, 1995, image, Sergeant Spradlin can be seen calmly managing the checkpoint in his easy-going manner. Other TPD personnel from left to right are Officer Phil Bendik, Sgt. Dexter Nelms, Officer Dave Koenig, Officer Marsha Barnet, and Officer Joe Simpson.

The department's communication center supports TPD's officers and serves the citizens of Torrance with innovation and professionalism. This 1996 image shows, from left to right, the following: (front row) dispatcher Robin Glenn, Rich Silagy, Lt. Emilio Paerels, and dispatcher Pam Shaw; (second row) Sgt. Ron Traber, Bruce Bott, Larry Davis, Bill Ferrell, George Morales, dispatcher Debbie Rogers, dispatcher Rose Fernandez, dispatcher Kathy Diaz, Tim Stark, Karl Young, and Sgt. Ralph Blount.

Seen in 1996 are forgery detectives Barry Walsh (left) and Vic Grijalva just prior to serving an arrest warrant somewhere in Los Angeles County.

The police department manages over 100 vehicles, both marked and unmarked, all of which are prepared and maintained by the city's fleet services department. For many years, services officer Earnest "Ernie" Peterman was the heart and soul of the motor transport section. He can be seen here in 1996 about to take a Chevrolet Caprice to the yard.

Upon Chief DeLadurantey's resignation in March 1997, Capt. James Herren was appointed acting chief. He was subsequently appointed chief of police on August 19, 1997. Chief Herren joined TPD on September 30, 1974. New initiatives instituted during his tenure were the bicycle detail, detective economic crimes section, forensic computer lab, police cadet program, emergency services detail, and the animal control section. Chief Herren was born in the South Bay. He selflessly donated countless hours of his personal time in order to enhance the level of professionalism in law enforcement. He retired on August 27, 2006, after providing 32 years of dedicated service to the city of Torrance.

December 26, 1999, was Sgt. Ron Ingram's last day at work, culminating a career that began on November 8, 1971. He is seen here (center) with, from left to right, (first row) dispatchers Dana Lukas, Taunja Chang, and Tara Jackson; (second row) dispatcher Pam Shaw, former sergeant Bob Such (retired in 1985), and dispatcher Debbie Rogers.

Seen in this May 2000 image are, from left to right, (first row) Sgt. Brad Wilson, Lt. Dennis Addington, and Sgt. Kevin Kreager; (second row) Sgt. Lloyd Degonia, Sgt. Mark Hein, Lt. John Neu, and Officer Keith Thompson.

In this staged 2003 image, Officer Jennifer Uyeda is seen in foot pursuit of a burglary "suspect."

Starting in October 2000, all community lead officers as well as those officers assigned to the mall detail have to complete a police bicycle course. Bicycles offer a quick and efficient means of patrolling parks, schools, alleys, and shopping areas. In addition to routine patrol, bicycle detail officers participate in a number of special events, such as the Fourth of July celebration at Wilson Park, the Armed Forces Day parade, and bicycle rodeos at local elementary schools. In this image, bicycle detail officers Jeff Livingston (left) and Ed Galang are seen during the 2005 Armed Forces Day parade.

California Peace Officers' memorial ceremonies have been conducted in the state capitol since 1977. The ceremonies honor those officers who have fallen in the line of duty the preceding year, recognizing the sacrifice of those loved and left behind. This 2006 image shows TPD honor guard members, from left to right, Sgt. Steve Bock, Officer Jeremiah Hart, Officer Chad Farley, and Officer Dusty Garver in front of the California Peace Officers Memorial at Tenth Street and Capitol Mall in Sacramento. Members of the honor guard are the only officers authorized to wear the campaign hats.

Motorcycle officer Dusty Garver is seen during the 2006 Armed Forces Day parade. Dusty, a former staff sergeant in the U.S. Marine Corps, could not resist in joining some active-duty U.S. Marines in performing push-ups in front of the grand stand—once a U.S. Marine, always a U.S. Marine.

ACROSS AMERICA, PEOPLE ARE DISCOVERING SOMETHING WONDERFUL. *THEIR HERITAGE.*

Arcadia Publishing is the leading local history publisher in the United States. With more than 4,000 titles in print and hundreds of new titles released every year, Arcadia has extensive specialized experience chronicling the history of communities and celebrating America's hidden stories, bringing to life the people, places, and events from the past. To discover the history of other communities across the nation, please visit:

www.arcadiapublishing.com

Customized search tools allow you to find regional history books about the town where you grew up, the cities where your friends and family live, the town where your parents met, or even that retirement spot you've been dreaming about.